Teach Yourself Piano

Sugabsen Martins Dajangla

© 2015 Sugabsen Martins Dajangla

All rights reserved. No part of this publication may be reproduced, stored in a retrieval system or transmitted in any form or by any means, electronic, mechanical, photocopying, recording or otherwise without the prior permission of the author.

Printed by
SETS computers S
angassumi, Ganye
Adamawa State.
07061981191

DEDICATION

This book is dedicated to the Federation of Lutheran Youth Bands (FELY Bands) and to my parents, Hon. And Mrs. Martins Dajangla Nyitu of blessed memory.

CHAPTER ONE

Introduction

Time without number I have been approached by people that I should teach them how to play the Piano especially when they see me or hear me play. I could not figure out why, because, obviously, I do not consider myself a star player, there are many people that play the piano more than I. I know that I cannot at the same time teach all the people that request for me to teach them the piano so; I decided to write this handbook in your hand now. This is my own way of teaching them. This small handbook is practical based, straight to the point and no- nonsense approach to playing the piano.

I have been playing the piano for sixteen years now so I believe I am capable of adding to someone's knowledge of the piano. All the mistakes you may encounter (if any), in this write up are mine. This small book is a powerful tool packaged with a lot of information that will make you realise your dream of playing the piano or at least adding to your knowledge of the piano. It is good for beginners and intermediates, and church pianists. In order to avoid overload of information, this book will be in series and this is the first in the series.

CHAPTER TWO

Classification of Musical Instruments

The understanding and knowledge of musical instruments which is a basic issue of concern to us at this moment will better be achieved when we look at what **Music** is all about. What then is music?

Music can simply be defined as the arrangement, organisation or combination of sound in a pleasing manner which makes meaning to the ear when sung as well as played on a musical instrument.

There are four categories of musical instruments which include the following:

1. Strings
2. Wood Wind
3. Brass
4. Percussion

1. Stringed instruments

    These are type of musical instruments fixed with strings and played by plugging with finger or a bow. e.g. Violin, Guitar, Viola, etc.

2. Wood Wind instruments

    These are a category of musical instruments which are mostly made of metal or wood and are played by blowing. e.g. Flute, Recorder, Clarinet etc.

3. Brass Instruments

    These are musical instruments that are made of only brass (a very light yellow shiny metal) and are also played by blowing. e.g. Trumpet, Trombone, Saxophone, etc.

4. Percussion instruments

   These kind of musical instruments are played either by striking, beating or tapping. e.g. Drums, **Piano**, Cymbal, Xylophone, Conga etc.

Notwithstanding, our major concern is the piano. Before we go into what playing the piano is all about, it is necessary that we create a distinction between these two similar instruments which many people cannot differentiate from each other. It is the Keyboard and the Piano.

Differences between Keyboard and Piano

Keyboard	Piano
electronic	it is non-electronic
Large	Larger with more octaves compared to the keyboard
Can be programmed to produce sound of a range of musical instruments which come as voices e.g. guitar, flute, xylophone	Cannot be programmed to produced any sound other than the piano sound which is voice 001 on most keyboards
easily mobile	Immobile
Usually comes with sound tracks and Can be used to sequence sound	Does not come with sound tracks and cannot sequence sound tracks

| tracks | |

Having known the differences, throughout this series, I shall be using piano to mean the keyboard since the principles guiding their play is the same.

Fundamental Approach to Piano

Better understanding is gained if we begin by following certain steps that will finally take us to our expected target. This can be possible only when we start by discovering the elementary ideas governing the Piano since we know that the foundation of anything matters a lot.

One of such fundamental variables is the solfa notation. Solfa notation is the method of representing musical notes with short words. There are seven (7) of them. They are

doh, re, mi, fah, soh, lah, te, doh^{l}

The last doh written as (doh^{l}) with a prime or a superscript is repetition of the first (doh). It is known in music that any group or set of eight (8) notes considered together is called an **Octave**.

Keys

Actually, there are twelve (12) keys in music which are represented by seven alphabets of the abc as follows (A – B – C – D – E – F – G). When you count the alphabets, they are seven in number the remaining five are either sharps or flats. They are as follows

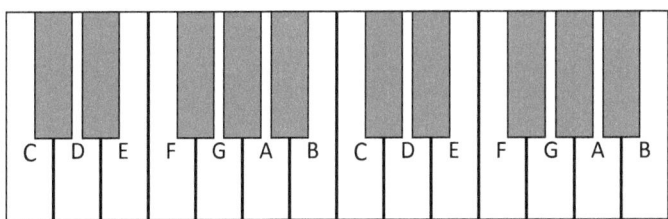

Notice that the same set of seven notes repeat themselves over and over again. That is, the notes sound the same but different pitches. For example, if you play a C and move to the right until you find the next C, you will notice that if you play them simultaneously, both notes sound the same but one is higher than the other. The remaining five are the set of black keys, they are five in number and they keep on reoccurring throughout.

These five notes can be named as sharps (#) or flats (b).
Sharp: sharp is a name given to the black key directly to the right of a white key.
Flat: it is a name given to the black key directly to the left of a white key

e.g.

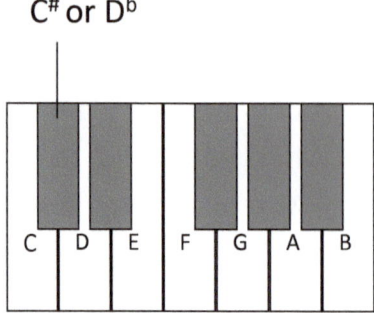

The arrow shows C♯ (C sharp) when you count it from the left and it is D♭ when you count it from the right. Therefore we can say that the black keys have two names either a sharp or a flat.

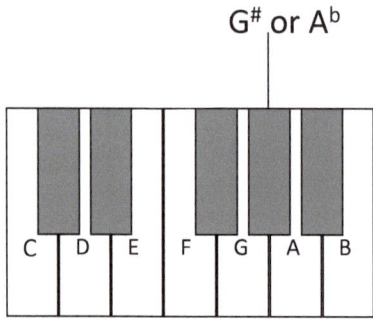

This example above shows (G sharp) which can also be called (A flat)

Principle of Diatonic Scale

The principle of diatonic scale gives us a clue or an idea of the relationship that exist in the solfa notation as follows:

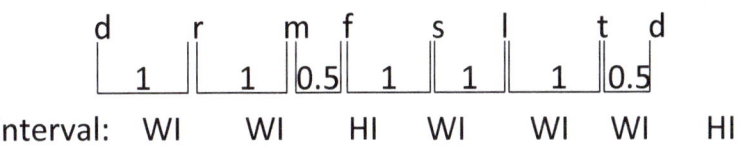

Interval: WI   WI   HI   WI   WI   WI   HI

WI Stands for Whole Interval and
HI Stands for Half interval

What it means is that from every
doh to reh is a whole interval
reh to me is a whole interval
me to fah is a half interval
fah to soh is a whole interval
soh to la is a whole interval
la to te is a whole interval
te to doh¹ is a half interval

This can be memorised as whole, whole, half, whole, whole, whole, half intervals. Tonally it will be memorised as tone, tone, semitone, tone, tone, tone, and semitone.

What is an interval?
In music an interval is a distance in pitch between two notes. The interval is counted from lower to higher note with the lower counted as one (1).

What is a whole step?

In playing the piano from note to note, when you skip one note, you are said to have made a whole interval movement.

e.g

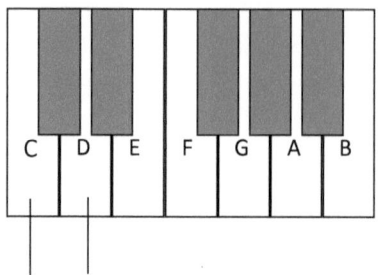

When you play from C to D as indicated by the arrows, you have made a whole interval movement. This is so because you have skipped the black note in between them which is C (sharp). Notice the whole interval movement made above is from a white note to a white note. It should be noted that the whole interval movement can be from a black to a black note as illustrated below

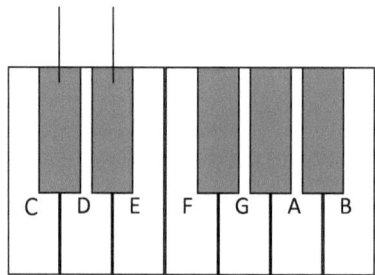

From the above, the first black note $C^{\#}$ or D^{b} to the immediate next black note $D^{\#}$ or E^{b} is a whole interval movement you are skipping key D (that is) the white note in between them. As a general rule, anytime you skip a note you have made a whole interval movement.

Half Interval

When you do not skip any note on the piano but play from a note to the next immediate neighbouring note, you are making a half interval movement. This can be seen as follows:

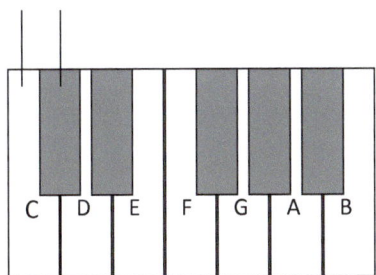

You have seen that the movement is from the first white note (C) to the immediate next note (C# or D♭). That kind of movement is a half interval movement because we did not skip any note. This can also begin from a black note to a white note as follows:

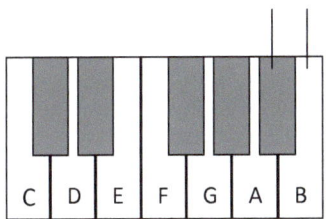

Here, it begins on a black note (A# or B♭) to a white note B unlike the first one which began on a white note.

Identifying Keys on the Piano

As a foundation let us talk about how you can memorise the notes on the Piano.

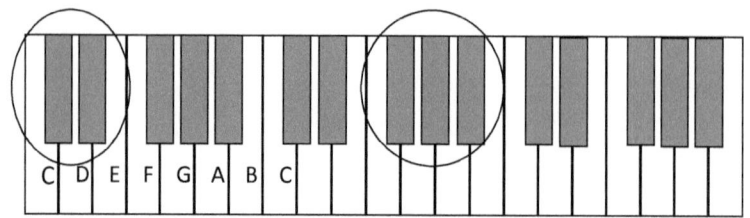

C is located directly to the bottom-left of the two grouped black keys while F is located directly to the bottom-left of the three grouped black keys. For the black keys, it has earlier been explained that they bear the name sharp or flat.

When you observe the Piano in ascending order its arrangement is like these:

CC#, DD#, E, FF#, GG#, AA#, B (ascending order)

In the same vein when the Piano is observed from a descending order, the following picture is got

BB♭, AA♭, GG♭, F, EE♭, DD♭, C (descending order)

Do you know that the arrangement might be confusing? But let us look at a simple principle there. While C and F have sharps, they have no flats and on the other hand, B and E have flats but do not have sharps. Another way to memorise the notes of the Piano can be seen below:

S/N	Specific name	Colour indication of the key	Symbol of the key
1.	C natural	White	C
2.	C sharp or D flat	Black	C#
3.	D natural	White	D
4.	D sharp or E flat	Black	D#
5.	E natural	White	E
6.	F natural	White	F
7.	F Sharp or G flat	Black	F#
8.	G natural	White	G
9.	G Sharp or A flat	Black	G#
10.	A natural	White	A
11.	A Sharp or B flat	Black	A#
12.	B natural	White	B

Natural means a key that is not sharp or flat. It is written just the alphabet without any sign of Sharp or flat. The natural is not written along with the alphabet but the alphabet alone.

e.g. is not written as C natural but simply C.

CHAPTER THREE

Melodic Interval

In this chapter we shall see how we can view the Piano in terms of playing melodic interval. We already know what an interval is (both whole and half). Now, let's get into business.

Intervals are said to be melodic when they are sounded separately. The major diatonic scale (solfa) can be played as seen below

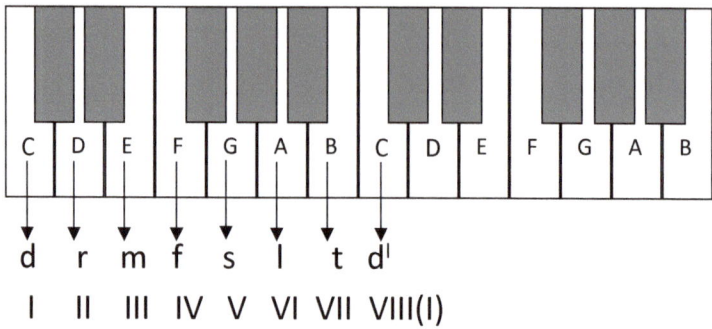

I am sure by now you know that the 8th note is a repetition of the first note to make it an octave (set of eight notes). This solfa is obtained using the principle of major diatonic scale. Supposing we want to play the solfa on key D, the illustration is shown below.

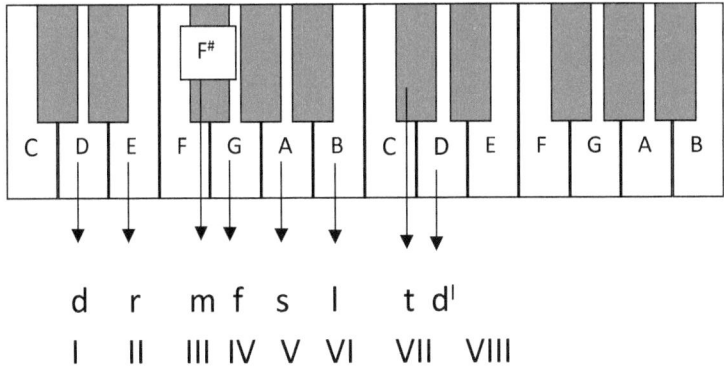

When you observe the interval between the notes, you will realise that it is the diatonic scale which is shown below

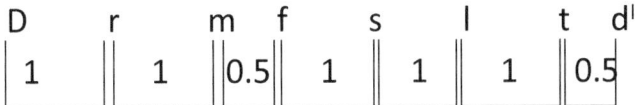

You should find out and play the melodic interval exercise on all the twelve keys of music.

CHAPTER FOUR

Harmonic Intervals

Having known melodic interval there is need for you to know the harmonic interval which will eventually lead us to the formation of chords. We shall now talk about some important variables which will lead us to that.

Perfect and major intervals

An interval between keynote (tonal centre) or tonic of a major scale and the unison, 4th, 5th, or octave of that scale is called **Perfect interval.**

For example, the difference between C to G (in a C major scale) is called **Perfect 5th interval.** This is illustrated below

Perfect intervals

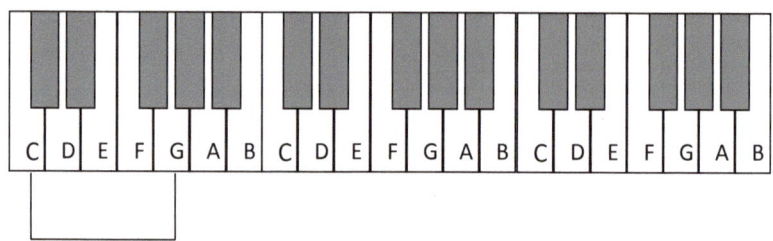

Perfect 5th interval

The difference between C to F is called Perfect 4th as seen below

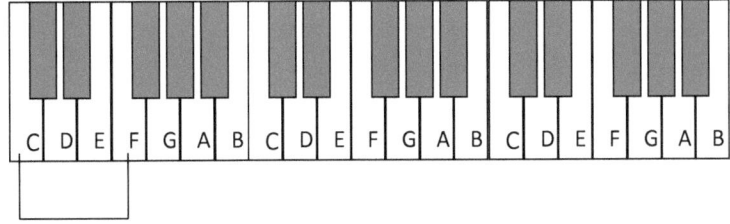

Perfect 4th interval

The difference from C to C¹ is called perfect octave. It is demonstrated below

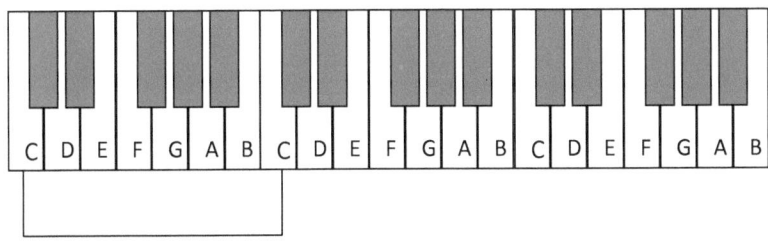

Perfect octave

The difference between C to the same C is called Perfect unison. It is shown below

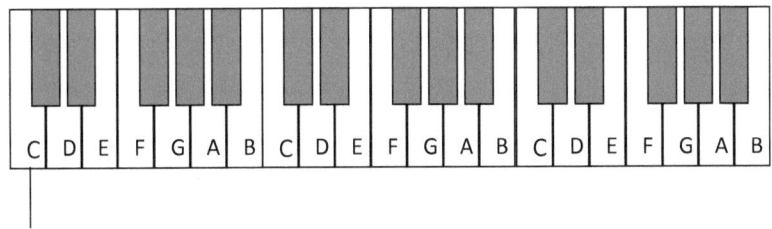

Perfect unison

Major Intervals

The interval between the keynotes (tonal centre) or tonic of a major scale and the 2nd, 3rd, 6th, or 7th of that scale is called a Major interval

For example, the difference from C to D (in a C major scale) is called major 2nd interval. It is shown below

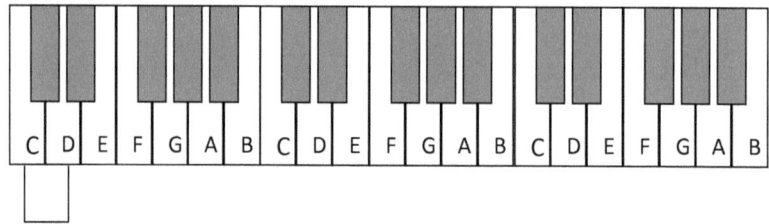

Major 2nd Interval

The difference from C to E is called major 3rd interval. It is shown below

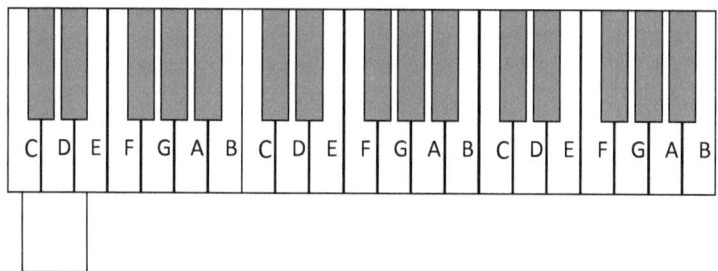

Major 3rd interval

The difference between C to A is called major 6th interval. This is shown below

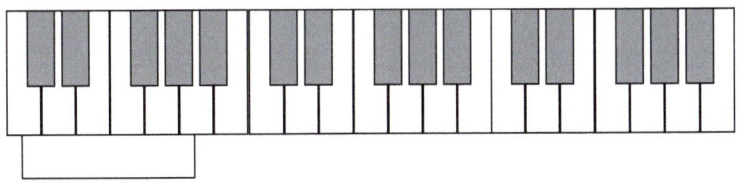

Major 6th interval

The difference between C to B is called major 7th interval. It is given as shown below

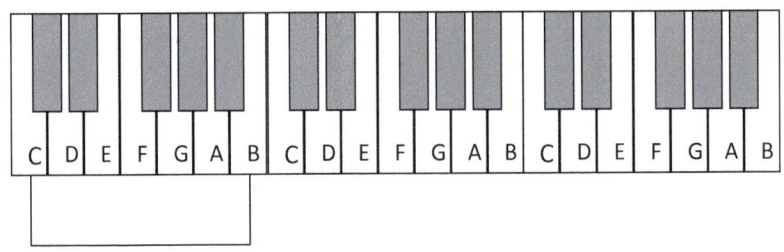

Major 7th interval

Summary of Intervals

Perfect Intervals	Major Intervals
Unison	2nd
4th	3th
5th	6th
Octave	7th

CHAPTER FIVE

Chords

There are many categories or classes of chords such as major triad chords, minor triad chords, diminish triad chords, major seventh chords, dominant seventh chords, diminish seventh chords, minor seventh chords, major ninth chords, minor ninth chords, dominant ninth chords, major eleventh chords, minor eleventh chords, dominant eleventh chords, major thirteenth chords, minor thirteenth chords, dominant thirteenth chords, and altered chords. Here, we shall be discussing on major triad, which is very elementary and foundational.

Primary and Major Triads

The most important triads of a key are founded or built on 1st, 4th, and 5th scale degrees of the major scale. An example is shown below

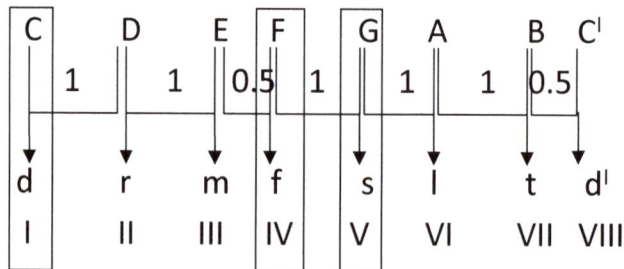

These three above I, IV and V are called the **primary triads** or primary chords and are identified by the Roman numerals as above.

Tones in the Major Scale

For example the C Major scale is C – D – E – F – G – A – B – C'. Out of the eight (8) notes (excluding the perfect octave C') three of them are primary or **Major triads.**
C is one of them
C = (C + E + G), the next one is
F = (F + A + C) and the last one is
G = (G + B + D).
You will learn in the next book that C –Ⓓ –Ⓔ – F – G –Ⓐ – Ⓑ – C' the ones circled are associated with either minor or diminish.

The primary triad are major triads because they consist of the root (tonic), a Major 3rd and a perfect 5th.

Major 3rd interval

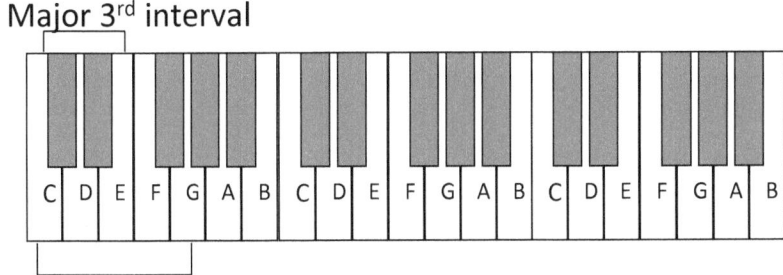

Perfect 5th interval

The above diagram displays a major triad chord in the key of C. The chord pictured above is known as C Major Triad chord. Since the fourth and the fifth degree are also major triads, they are called F major and G major respectively. That brings us to a very key statement that (the appropriate combination of perfect fifth and Major third with reference to the root (tonic) will give a Major chord).

> FORMULAE: MAJOR THIRD + PERFECT FIFTH = MAJOR CHORD

Let us try to form the Major chord on key F using the formula we have.

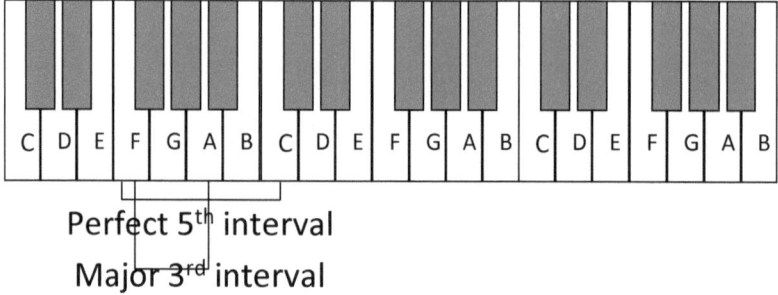

Perfect 5th interval
Major 3rd interval

When you add them together you will find F + A + C which is the F Major chord. Let us also consider forming C#/ D♭

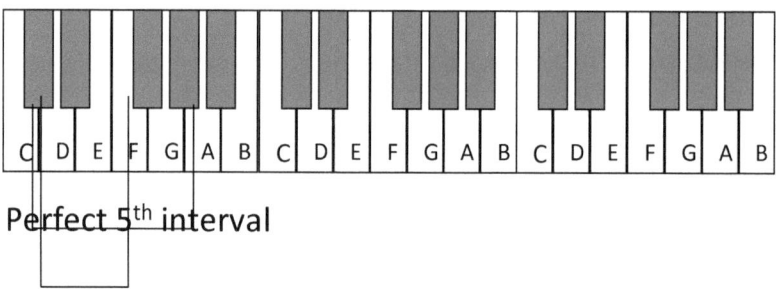

Perfect 5th interval

Major 3rd interval

When put together, it is C# + F + G# which is the C# Major chord. If you can memorise the formulae, it means that anytime you are approached, you can demonstrate the major chords in music. This is so, owing to the fact that
Major third = 4 half intervals or steps from the root
Perfect fifth = 7 half intervals or steps from the root

Now, here is more to it. Let us say we want to build a G Major chord
1. Start at G (the root)
2. Add a Major third (4 half steps/intervals) from the root
3. Add a perfect fifth (7 half steps/intervals) from the root position, you will end up with G + B + D as your G Major chord.

In the key of C the
I(d) triad (or chord) is the C triad (C – E – G)
IV(f) triad (or chord) is the F triad (F – A – C)
V(s) triad (or chord) is the G triad (G + B + D)

C Major Scale

C	D	E	F	G	A	B	C¹
E			A	B			
G			C	D			

In form of solfa it will be like these

d	r	m	f	s	l	t	d¹
m			l	t			
s			d	r			

These chords I, IV, V or the doh, fah, and soh are the major chords.

With these, you are good to start practicing your Major chords. In the next edition you will learn chord inversion, minor intervals and many more, therefore, watch out for the next in series. Below are some songs you can use to start practicing. Practice these songs on all the twelve keys.

```
I     IV    I      V           I
```
1. Oh Lord my God, how excellent is your name
```
      IV   I      V            I
```
   In all the earth, how excellent is your name


```
         I           IV         V           I
```
2. Holy spirit   Holy spirit Holy spirit Holy spirit (2X)

```
         I                    IV          V
```
   You are welcome, You are welcome You are welcome
   You are welcome (2X)


```
         I           I          IV           I
```
3. Kayi Magana kawai ya Yesu kayi Magana kawai

```
         I           I          IV           V
```
   Ban isaba kazo wurinaba kayi Magana kawai


```
         I           I          IV           I
```
   Kayi Magana kawai ya Yesu kayi Magana kawai

```
         I    IV         V               I
```
   Ban isaba kazo wurinaba kayi Magana kawai

List of Words and their meaning

Chord: two or more musical notes played together or sung simultaneously.

Flat: pitched one half-step below a particular note

Interval: the musical distance between the pitches of two notes

Melody: the linear structure of a piece of music in which single notes follow one another.

Octave: an interval between two notes consisting of eight notes inclusive or seven steps on the diatonic scale

Pitch: to set a musical instrument to a particular key

Scale: a series of musical notes, usually sequential, arranged in ascending or descending order of pitch.

Sharp: higher in pitch by half step

Tonic (root): The first note of a musical scale and the harmony built on this note.

Unison: two notes sharing the same pitch

Triad: a musical chord consisting of three notes, especially a chord made up of a tonic, a third, and a fifth.

www.ingramcontent.com/pod-product-compliance
Lightning Source LLC
Chambersburg PA
CBHW040304220526
45473CB00002B/577